COASTAL SHIPPING

OF THE ISLE of MAN

1946 ~ present day

STAN BASNETT

To Richard on your special birthday

Stan Basnett

Published on the Isle of Man by
Lily Publications, PO Box 33, Ramsey, Isle of Man IM99 4LP
Tel: +44 (0)1624 898446   Fax: +44 (0)1624 898449
E-mail: info@lilypublications.co.uk   Web: www.lilypublications.co.uk

Ramsey Steamship Co.'s *ss Ben Vooar 2* at Douglas. (photo the late W.A. Mackie)

I have always had an interest in the sea and ships largely due to my grandfather's influence on me as a young boy. My interest in photography of ships evolved from that and was encouraged in my teens by an elderly member of the Isle of Man Photographic Society, Bill Mackie, who was a keen amateur photographer and had been the local manager of the Lancashire Associated Collieries. His job brought him into close contact with vessels used in importing coal to the island. One of his photographs prefaces this introduction.

The Isle of Man, for those who don't already know, is a self governing Crown Dependency. It is 50 km long and 21km wide with an area of 572 sq.km. It is situated in the middle of the Irish Sea and now has a population of just over 80,000, although at the start of the period covered by this book, it stood at around 40,000.

In the Victorian and Edwardian eras the island developed as a holiday destination for the working classes from the north west of England and 'sail away to the Isle of Man' became the slogan for the newly emerging tourist industry destined to become the mainstay of the island's economy but with farming and fishing providing the only all year round employment The dependency on tourism led to a 'boom and bust' economy which resulted in a migration of young people from the island.

After the Second World War and coming into the period covered by this book, the island hoped that the tourist industry would continue as before. It was not to be and, as with many other seaside resorts in the British Isles, it entered a period of decline. Farming and fishing, on the other hand, remained much as before.

The Manx Government looked for an alternative economic base and although forays were made into the introduction of light industry with limited success, it was not the answer. It was dependent on the import of raw material and the export of the

The *ss Ben Vooar 2* discharging coal at the Raglan Pier Port Erin. (Stan Basnett collection)

finished product which resulted in the businesses becoming uncompetitive, even with generous tax concessions.

The answer came in the form of financial services and banking which once again set the island on its feet. That is a subject for separate study, suffice to say that being an island with no significant natural resources, it depends to a large extent, on imported goods for almost all of its activity.

The island's capital and principal port is Douglas with Ramsey in the north of the island being second in importance. Other ports are Peel on the west coast, Port Erin, Port St Mary and Castletown in the south and the small port of Laxey on the east coast between Douglas and Ramsey now closed to commercial traffic; but at one time it was the centre of the export of lead, silver and zinc from the lucrative Laxey mines but by the 1930s its traffic was limited to coal and grain for the local flour mills. All of the island's ports except Port Erin and

Port St Mary evolved around the mouth of a river.

Douglas harbour has migrated seawards since the natural inlet at the mouth of the Douglas river was first used as a haven for the local fishing fleet. It is hard to appreciate now that the harbour started in the area known as 'The Lake' which is now occupied by the railway station and a supermarket.

By 1700, in response to demand a pier was constructed, which became known as 'The Tongue' and the harbour commenced its march seawards with stone quay walls built on either side of the inlet as the town of Douglas grew. The tidal harbour was finished when the Red Pier was completed in 1891.

The demand for increased berthage at all states of the tide soon followed driven by an increase in commercial traffic and tourism. So by the end of the next century a breakwater had been built and a low water landing pier. They were eventually named

The Isle of Man Steam Packet coaster *ss Conister* at the Red Pier berth Douglas on 7th March 1964 prior to departure and ready to load hides from the abattoir which were carried on the hatch covers and discharged at Birkenhead lairage - last on first off! I never tire of looking at this picture and I can still hear the sounds and smell the oily steam and of course those hides.

An unidentified Ramsey Steamship vessel discharging coal at Peel East Quay. (Stan Basnett collection)

the Battery Pier and the Queen Victoria Pier respectively, the latter being completed in 1891.

Still the demand continued and by 1936 works to construct an extension to the Red Pier into deep water had been completed becoming the King Edward Pier. A viaduct to connect it to the Victoria Pier and avoid the commercial part of the harbour was also constructed at the same time.

The advent of Ro-Ro services to the island resulted in larger vessels using the port which in turn, required linkspan facilities, deepening of the berths and a marshalling area to be constructed. The Battery Pier was, by this time providing inadequate protection for the outer harbour and a new breakwater was built and completed in 1983.

The inner harbour has become a marina and is no longer open to commercial traffic. Part of the harbour has been filled to provide boat and car parking and the once busy quayside is now being pedestrianised as the harbour continues it's

relentless migration seaward. That is the position at the end of yet another century. It begs the question as to where it will be in another one hundred years! To a lesser extent Peel harbour has followed a similar trend but Ramsey, Castletown and Port St Mary have remained much the same. The other ports are closed to commercial traffic.

A number of island based shipping companies have existed at various times, but two in particular have stayed the course. The Isle of Man Steam Packet Co. founded in 1830 and the Ramsey Steamship Co. dating from 1913. The former concentrating on passenger services and break bulk general cargo and the latter entirely on bulk cargo.

It all changed with the advent of containerised goods traffic, started by the Steam Packet and expanded by IOM Ferry Express, which inevitably led to the introduction of a Ro-Ro service in 1972; even though it was late compared to the rest of the British Isles, all of which is well documented

On passage with the *ss Ben Ain* of the Ramsey Steamship Co. (photo the late W.A. Mackie)

elsewhere. It was inevitable and the consequence was that coastal shipping to the island that was already on the decline almost completely vanished.

Even though coal and timber imports would eventually be brought to the island almost entirely on road vehicles and Ro-Ro vessels, there are other commodities that still require transport in bulk. Fuel oils and other petroleum products arrive by coastal tanker and cement is transported in bulk. Tankers still handle some LPG products, notwithstanding that natural gas is now piped to the island.

Against all odds, a shipping company, Mezeron Ltd., was set up in 1983 to handle general cargo, both break bulk and in containers, to service small businesses and it continues to

thrive in the face of competition.

The story of how the import of goods by sea was carried out and how it has changed over the last fifty years is told in pictures. It is a personal view and all of the pictures, unless otherwise acknowledged, have been taken by me. The accelerated pace of change that has taken place is nowhere better illustrated than at Douglas, where commercial shipping has migrated from the inner tidal harbour, now a marina, to the outer harbour.

Here then are the photographs, loosely grouped in date order, each presenting a snapshot in time of a recent way of life that has gone forever. Look closely and you will see other interesting details in the photographs which, I hope, will set you reminiscing.

This photograph dates from September 1962 when coal was still a major import to the island. This view of Douglas harbour shows the **ss Ben Maye** discharging coal for the domestic market probably to the order of a local coal merchant or several who may have joined to make a full load. The **ss Rockville** formerly the **ss Orenie** built in 1922 and belonging to J.S.Monk Ltd of Liverpool, with fuel for the coal fired power station at Pulrose, was one of the largest steam coasters to use the inner harbour.

Douglas inner harbour again and two of Ramsey Steamship Co. vessels discharging coal. **ss Ben Veen 1** (formerly the **ss Crossbill**) one of the last steamers operated by the company and the **mv Ben Vooar 3** (formerly the **mv Mudo**) which was the second motor vessel which they acquired in 1959.

The **ss Ben Maye** (formerly the **ss Kyle Rea**) seen discharging at the North Quay in Douglas using the Harbour Board Ransomes and Rapier cranes. Once again the cargo is coal and is being discharged into lorries by hand loaded tubs in the hold by the local dockworkers who were always known as coal heavers.

Whilst I have deliberately avoided much of the Isle of Man Steam Packet Co movements in this book as they have been well recorded elsewhere, I can't really ignore their break bulk cargo vessels which were very much part of the island shipping scene in bringing cargo to the island. This photo of the **ss Peveril (2)** was taken as it backs off the Battery Pier having discharged a heavy load at the crane berth.

Every Christmas the Steam Packet Co cargo vessels traditionally berthed in the inner harbour over the holiday period secure from any gales thrown at the island, particularly easterlies, at that time. Here is the **ss Conister (1)** and the **mv Peveril** the third vessel of the company to carry the name.

This evocative photograph of the **ss Conister (1)** was taken in 1964 leaving Douglas almost at the end of her long career with the Isle of Man Steam Packet Co. She was the last single hatch steam coaster operating in the Irish Sea and was scrapped in 1965.

The Ramsey Steamship Co. took delivery of another motor vessel in 1963. It was built by E.J.Smit of Westerbrook in Holland and was six weeks late in delivery due to an extremely severe winter. The photograph, which was given to me by Captain Louis Cormode, shows him standing on the ice beside the ship. It was named **mv Ben Varrey** and became the third vessel to carry the name. All of the Ramsey Steamship Co. vessels carried Manx Gaelic names, all prefixed by the word Ben meaning 'woman'. Ben Varrey literally means 'woman of the sea' or 'colloquially mermaid'.

One of the unusual imports to the island was explosives for quarrying and they were imported through Ramsey and handled by Lenny Simpson who was the ICI agent on the island.

Here we see *mv Lady Roslin* arriving on 4th February 1965 on the top of the tide and, after discharge of what was usually only a relatively small quantity of material, would leave almost immediately. These vessels were always immaculate and at the time the photograph was taken it was seven years old. Imagine what the scene would be like today with the plethora of Health and Safety regulations that seem to invade every aspect of our lives.

An idyllic shot of Douglas harbour as it was in the sixties looking from the North Quay across the inner harbour to the outer harbour with the *mv Staley Bridge* and one of the Ben boats berthed on the North Quay. A coaster is coming in on the tide and passing the *ss Peveril* on the Steam Packet Berth, or to use its older name, the Office Berth.

This photograph of the two hatch Dublin registered steam coaster *ss Loch Linnie* was taken at Peel Breakwater in 1959 when it called for water. The vessel was owned by V.Nolan Ltd. of Dublin and dated from 1928.

The small coastal tanker *mt Eileen M* belonging to Metcalf Motor Coasters was a regular visitor to Douglas discharging aviation spirit for Shell and Manx Petroleums alongside the Approach Road which was not closed to traffic during discharge! Another horror by modern day standards but one which was successfully carried out without incident.

One of the few exports from the island in recent times was seed potatoes. The Board of Agriculture, as it was known then, ran a research establishment at Knockaloe and provided a service to Manx farmers to ensure disease free potatoes and what you see here is the manually intensive system of loading. I am not sure if it was good for the potatoes!

In 1964 Douglas Gasworks were still producing town gas from coal, but the conversion to gas production from petroleum products started in the same year. It was to signal the end of the import of bulk coal to the island. On the 24th April *mt Regitze Tholstrup* was the first lpg tanker to come to the island and is seen discharging at the Tongue in the inner harbour. It is incredible now to think that the vessel sat on the bottom after discharge, virtually in the centre of town, prior to departure on the next tide. It was all to change after a tragic accident in Spain involving a road tanker alerted the world to the dangers of handling butane and propane,

At this time coastal shipping was very much the province of the Dutch and the island saw many Dutch coasters either on charter to UK firms or bringing cargo direct from foreign ports. Here the Dutch coaster *mv Lydia*, registered in Heerenveern, is discharging bagged cement at the Coffee Palace Berth at Douglas for one of the local builders merchants.

Also located within the inner harbour at Douglas was the Esso fuel depot and again, the tankers, during discharge, would sit on the harbour bed until the next tide. This view of the *mt Esso Ottawa* was taken in December 1964 alongside what was known as the Wigan Berth, which was adjacent to their storage tanks.

Many lpg tankers belonging to A/S Kosan came to the island and gradually got bigger over the years. This is the *mt Annette Holstrup* in the process of discharging at the Tongue. These liquefied gas tankers, were only 300 tons, which was ideal for the restricted dimensions on the berth at the Tongue.

There were two vessels within the Nobel Division of ICI and both, on occasion, visited the island to discharge explosives, This is the **mv Lady McGowan,** the slightly older of the two, dating from 1952. Both were about 700 ton and slightly larger than the Isle of Man Steam Packet Co's vessel **mv Ramsey,** which was designed specifically for the break bulk cargo service between Liverpool and Ramsey.

A regular visitor to the island in the 60s was the **mv Indorita,** a small 200 ton coaster owned by Coppack Bros of Connahs Quay since 1946. Its hull form could not disguise the fact that it was from an earlier time having been built in 1920 for John Summers & Sons. It would carry almost any cargo to the island and would be fortunate enough to get a return load of scrap metal now and again. It was powered by a Bolingers 2cylinder oil engine

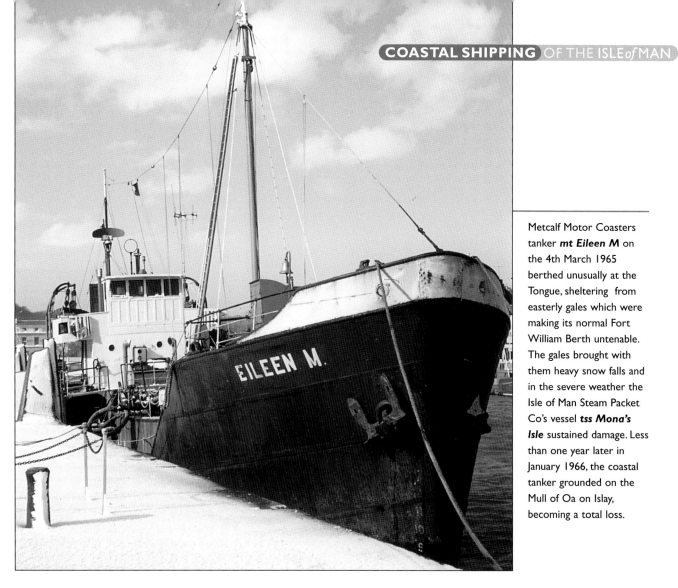

Metcalf Motor Coasters tanker **mt Eileen M** on the 4th March 1965 berthed unusually at the Tongue, sheltering from easterly gales which were making its normal Fort William Berth untenable. The gales brought with them heavy snow falls and in the severe weather the Isle of Man Steam Packet Co's vessel **tss Mona's Isle** sustained damage. Less than one year later in January 1966, the coastal tanker grounded on the Mull of Oa on Islay, becoming a total loss.

By way of complete contrast, at least weather wise, here is the Ramsey Steamship Co.'s **mv Ben Rein** (formerly the **mv Tomara**) discharging grain at Laxey for the Laxey Glen Flour Mills. The **Ben Rein** was the first motor vessel the company purchased in 1956 and heralded the demise of the steam coasters operated by the company. It was a move not welcomed by the island's small coal merchants because of the greater carrying capacity and difficulties financing and storing larger cargoes.

The *mv Ben Vooar 3* was the second motor vessel acquired by the Ramsey Steamship Co. in 1959. Formerly the Dutch registered **Mudo**, here it is berthed in the inner harbour at Port St. Mary in April 1965. Bulk deliveries of coal to the southern coal merchants was still a regular feature at this time. Later the port would see an upturn in traffic with the resurgence of the herring industry and later still with the export of scrap metal.

This photograph shows the *mv Hawarden Bridge* belonging to John Summers & Sons Ltd. of Shotton at Ramsey East Quay in June 1965. Summers small 300 ton coasters were regular visitors to the island and on this occasion the vessel was bringing bulk salt for the IOM Highway Board's northern depot for winter gritting. The island at this time still supported a healthy business in coach traffic and the picture warrants close inspection.

I hadn't realised until compiling this album of photographs that most seem to have been taken in the winter. It probably reflected the fact that there was more cargo traffic during the winter. Whatever the reason it gave me the opportunity to record these coasters in their proper environment. Here are two Dutch coasters arriving at Douglas in February 1966. The first is the *mv Zwartewater* followed by the *mv Saba*.

Here is the *mv Saba* entering Douglas. The vessel was Dutch registered and managed by Wijnne & Barends of Groningen. Much older than the *Zwartewater* it was built in Germany at Kiel in 1930.
I believe if my memory serves me right, that the vessel capsized and sank later after a cargo of steel shifted whilst on passage.

The *mt Mee Holstrup*, one of the smaller 300 ton liquefied gas tankers of the Trans Kosan Company is seen heading down the inner harbour at Douglas bound for Milford Haven. Robertsons *mv Jacinth* is at the Coffee Palace berth discharging coal for the power station.

In June 1966 it became apparent that something was going on in the Irish sea when a number of coasters appeared rigged with all manner of devices for scouring the sea bed. The first to arrive was the *mv Ceres* followed by vessels belonging to Gillie and Blair. It was the forerunner of the exploration that led to the formation of the Morecambe Bay and Liverpool Bay gas fields.

The *mv Glenfyne* at Port St. Mary on 15th December 1968. The vessel was one of the last 200 ton coasters to be
built for the Scottish Island's trade. Built in 1966 for Hay-Hamilton, by 1968 it was managed by Glenlight Shipping Ltd.

With the decline in the coal trade, it was inevitable that there would be a corresponding increase in the importation of lpg products and there followed a great variety of Trans-Kosan tankers carrying liquefied gas to Douglas. One of the more regular vessels employed was the *mt Helle Tholstrup* seen here turning in the upper reaches of the inner harbour, something that is hard to imagine now looking back some forty years.

Everards were still bringing coal for the power station which, despite continued modernisation to diesel generation, was still operating one steam turbine generating set. *mv Sonority* is approaching the inner harbour.

Qualtroughs of Castletown, a local timber merchant, almost every July would import a supply of timber for discharge at their local port. It was always a tight squeeze to enter the inner harbour and here the Danish coaster *mv Aase Hoj*, which was a frequent visitor to the island with timber, is entering the inner harbour in July 1966 with a load of timber from the port of Kemi in Finland. The reason that the timber was arriving in July was to avoid problems in Finland where the port was subject to winter icing.

Another photograph of *mv Hawarden Bridge* arriving at Douglas, the John Summers & Sons funnel insignia clearly visible. The vessel, at this time, was being managed by Coppacks of Connah's Quay.

The *mv Saint Ronan* approaching the Victoria Pier at Douglas in October 1968. The vessel was two years old and was one of two vessels owned by J. & A. Gardner at that time which had grey painted hulls with green boot topping. The rest of the fleet had black painted hulls with red boot topping.

BEN VOOAR

The *mv Ben Vooar 3* at Port St. Mary discharging coal by grab with the National Coal Board's mobile crane which will have travelled from Douglas for the purpose. In addition to the coal merchants mentioned earlier, there was a gas works at Port St. Mary which was still producing town gas from coal.

I mentioned earlier the resurgence of the herring fishery off the Isle of Man. Peel, Douglas and Port St. Mary were to see a huge increase in activity between 1967 and 1974 involving both fishing boats and coasters to carry the part processed fish to Europe and Scandinavia. The *mv Biscaya* of Dammers & Van de Heide's Shipping and Trading Co. arrived overnight in October 1968 at the Alfred Pier, Port St, Mary. It arrived late in the season to load the barrels of salted herring stacked on the pier.

A lively shot of the *mv Ben Rein* (the name meaning 'royal woman' or 'queen') as it leaves Douglas in ballast into a north easterly breeze. In the background is the newly built Sea Terminal. The roof over the restaurant earned the building the nickname of the 'lemon squeezer'. The lattice tower on the Victoria Pier is of interest as it housed the first harbour radar installation in the UK.

The *mv Ben Vooar 3* (the name means 'fat woman') is approaching the East Quay at Peel, this time with a cargo of road chippings from Northern Ireland.

I have included this photograph a little tongue in cheek. Is it the first Ro-Ro vessel to operate from the island? During the 1960's the Territorial Army were encouraged to the island for training exercises. The Royal Corps of Transport made several beach landings during the period and here the **HMAV Audemer** is loading vehicles off the beach at Peel in October 1968.

I did mention that most of my photographs seem to be taken in the winter months as this photograph of the Isle of Man Steam Packet Co.'s *mv Ramsey* arriving at Douglas shows. Although principally employed on the Liverpool/Ramsey route, the coaster did frequently use Douglas. Before the breakwater extension, entry to the port was always difficult with the wind from the easterly quadrant.

I have included this photograph of the *mv Ben Rein* because of its location. The vessel is berthed at Berth No.7 West, Quay Ramsey, also known as the grid iron berth. This enables the hull to be scraped and painted without the expense of dry docking or putting the ship on the slip at Ramsey as it is high and dry on the grid when the tide goes out. There is just sufficient access underneath for hull cleaning and painting. A little judicious repositioning allows all of the hull to be examined.

You might well ask what is going on here with the *mv Ben Varrey 3* apparently stuck across the entrance to the inner harbour at Douglas in choppy conditions with a following wind. Well, the answer is in the photograph below. The *mv Arnholt* is turning at the Coffee Palace berth preparing for departure and for some reason the **Ben Varrey** has entered the harbour too soon and a collision was narrowly avoided. The **Ben Varrey** secured at the Office Berth to allow the other coaster to leave.

Here the Dutch coaster *mv Arnholt* is photographed leaving Douglas into that freshening easterly gale with a rough passage ahead. Meanwhile, no doubt, the Harbour Master will be having some words with the master of the *mv Ben Varrey*.

I have included this photograph next because of its relevance to what happened with the *Arnholt*.. Here we see the *mv Rex* from the historic Dutch port of Appingedam arriving at Douglas with a load of timber which has shifted on passage. If you look at the semaphore signal on the Edward Pier the inner harbour is closed and yet the vessel is still proceeding inward. All a far cry from today's communication systems and harbour control.

The *mt Esso Brixham* is discharging at the Battery Pier, Douglas in July 1974 into Manx Petroleum's storage tanks. An arrangement had to made with the Shell distributer as the inner harbour depot belonging to Esso was no longer deemed safe due to its position in the town. Eventually, the Esso coastal tankers would stop deliveries to the island and a financial deal was made to service the Esso outlets through Manx Petroleums.

Another regular visitor to the island's ports was the Arklow registered *mv Avondale* owned by John Tyrrell and is seen here arriving at Douglas on a pleasant summers day with the crew out on deck ready to handle the mooring lines.

Continuing with the herring fishery, a number of specialised refrigerated vessels called at Port St. Mary for salt herring and here is another of Dammers & Van de Heide's vessels, the **mv Fedala** loading barrels at the end of the 1969 season before following the trade up the Scottish coast.

Another coaster bringing timber to one of the Douglas merchants was the German registered 400 ton **mv Tramp** which was photographed from the Approach Road passing the Isle of Man Steam Steam Packet Co.'s **mv Fenella** as it enters the inner harbour. What a great array of masts and derricks!

Douglas inner harbour at low water with the German coaster *mv Merwestad* discharging timber and the *mv Ben Veg* berthed outside the Douglas office of the Ramsey Steamship Co. awaiting orders.

We were to see the *mv Heathergate* much later on charter to the emergent Ronagency Shipping Co., but on this occasion, it is at Douglas for stores whilst working on drilling work in the Irish Sea in connection with gas exploration.

The *mv Ben Veg 2* was the fourth motor ship acquired by the Ramsey Steamship Co. and the second built exclusively for them. This time their new build had been in the UK at Clelands of Wallsend on Tyne in 1965. It is seen here in the inner harbour at Laxey where it was a frequent visitor with grain for the flour mills.

The large Swedish coaster *mv Bestic* arriving at Douglas on 17th December 1966 to load seed potatoes.

I promised that there would be more of the Kosan tankers and here is one of their 400 ton lpg tankers, the *mt Kitte Tholstrup*. Because their discharge berth was at the Tongue in the oldest part of the harbour with less depth of water available, they would always come and go on the top of the tide which meant that they would take the bottom during discharge. The new gas plant is visible in the background.

The Danish coaster *mv Hanne Scan* is loading seed potatoes at the Coffee Palace Berth on 25th October 1966. The berth was sometimes referred to by its older name the Double Corner. The Admiralty chart shows it as berth No.9 but now the whole of the inner harbour is closed to commercial traffic and is a water retained marina. The photograph was taken from the Isle of Man Steam Packet Co. Ltd catering department office - it is useful to have friends in high places!

The 500 ton coaster *mv Reginald Kearon* owned and operated by George Kearon of Arklow with a cargo of timber for the island. on 4th July 1969.

This is another of my favourite photographs as it so typifies a quiet late summer evening view of Douglas harbour in the sixties. It was taken in August 1969 and the Danish coaster *mv Gotha* has completed discharging a cargo of timber and is waiting for the tide whilst the "rowies", now very much a thing of the past, are all in for the night.

The *mv Ben Veg 2* at Castletown with the road swing bridge still in place and Castletown brewery still in operation.

Another view of the *mv Gotha* a little later than the photograph on the previous page, arriving with another load of timber on 1st July 1969. By the date of the arrival, the timber has come from one of the Finnish saw mills, probably at Kemi.

There is a good stiff easterly breeze pushing the *mv Janne Lindinger* up the harbour as it brings another cargo of timber for one of the two timber merchants at Douglas. Because of the sea conditions in the bay, the harbour pilot, Wally Shimmin, is seen boarding the coaster in the outer harbour. This photograph was taken in January 1967 and again, because of the time of year, it is more likely to have come from Noorkoping in Sweden.

Yet another "timber boat" once again at Douglas at the end of 1966. The Dutch registered 350 ton **mv Caravelle** having arrived with Swedish timber from one of the Baltic ports during winter storms. Many of these coasters were privately owned but were managed by one of the Dutch shipping agents, in this case by Wagenborg's Scheepvaart N.V.

The Dutch coaster **mv Lireco** was very much the mainstay of the IOM Ferry Express/Ronagency shipping Company when it started. In 1968 it finished its charter with them and was almost immediately back in familiar waters with a cargo of timber for Quiggin & Co., one of the local timber merchants.

This photograph of **ss Stormlight** leaving Douglas in an easterly swell in June 1968 clearly illustrates the size of these useful little coasters. They were designed for the Scottish Island trades but fiound useful employment in the Irish Sea. It was only 96ft long and was built for Ross Marshall of Greenock by Yarwoods in Northwich in 1957 and, even at that late period was built as a steam driven coaster.

It was finding gainful employment in the late sixties cable laying because it was steam driven hence the chute visible over the stern. It was laid up by Glenlight Shipping, awaiting conversion to diesel but eventually the vessel stranded on Jura, becoming a write-off.

Another small coaster which was a regular to the island and is included to show the difference between a 200 ton single hatch and a 300 ton twin hatch vessel. This is John Summer's **mv Staley Bridge** leaving Douglas. It would carry rock salt from Weston Point or chippings from Northern Ireland or indeed any other bulk cargo.

R. Cunningham of Belfast owned the 365 ton *mv Isle of Lewis* which was registered in Stornaway, seen here alongside Ramsey East Quay in 1967. It had just arrived on a Sunday and was waiting to load seed potatoes.

The German coaster *mv Stortebeker* at Ramsey in July 1969. Registered at Lubeck, the largest German port on the Baltic, it had finished discharging a load of timber and was ready to leave on the next tide.

Fuel oil for Peel Power Station was discharged at Peel breakwater through a heated pipe to the storage tanks some considerable distance from the point of discharge. Heavy oil was brought from Stanlow to the island by some regular visitors, one of which was the Swedish registered *mt Belinda*.

Whilst not strictly a coaster, I include this photograph for its interest value. Vessels due to dock at Liverpool would take a pilot off Point Lynas in Angelsey. However it was impossible in prolonged north-westerly gales for pilots to board from the pilot cutters and it was customary for the ships to shelter off the east coast of the island and the pilots to work there. Here, the **ss Wroclaw**, an elderly Baltic trader bringing timber to Liverpool, was short of water and being steam driven, it was essential that it came into Douglas for water. At the time it was arguably the longest vessel to enter the port.

Following the loss of the **mt Eileen M** Manx Petroleums had, through their agent, to find suitable small tankers capable of using the Fort William Berth. Metcalf Motor Coasters had some as did Christopher Rowbotham and Sons and in the event it was a vessel from the latter company that became the regular tanker. Here is the 290 ton **mt Rudderman** discharging at the berth.

Mention has already been made of the Liverpool Pilots operating off Douglas in the event of prolonged north-westerly gales making the pilot station off Point Lynas untenable. Here is the No.1 Liverpool Pilot boat *mv Sir Thomas Brockebank* off the back of the breakwater at Douglas. A pilot cutter has been launched to go to the Edward Pier to pick up pilots who have flown to the island from Liverpool.

SIR THOMAS BROCKLEBANK
MERSEY DOCKS & HARBOUR BOARD
1
LIVERPOOL

Because of its location in the middle of the Irish Sea shipping lanes, the island saw many coasters taking shelter from gales and it was not uncommon for vessels to enter port for adjustment to shifted cargo or for damage repair. By far the worst incident involved the coaster *mv Pointer*, operated by Link Lines Ltd., part of the Coast Lines Group. The vessel was photographed entering Douglas on the 21st November 1968. On passage from Northern Ireland, it had encountered heavy weather off the Point of Ayre developing a sixteen degree list due to part of its cargo of bacon sides shifting. It made the safe haven of Douglas and the following day was moved to the Battery Pier crane berth where the delicate operation of re-stowing took place. It didn't leave until the 24th November.

This time the *mv Aase Hoj*, which has already been shown threading its way into Castletown, is seen under way approaching Douglas. This photograph shows the lines of this typical coaster off to advantage. They really were the mainstay of the coasting fleet for almost two decades before vessels got bigger to compete with the emerging Ro-Ro traffic which was undermining the coastal trade.

The *mv Andreas Boye* was a regular visitor to the island with timber and here it is in Castletown harbour at the Umber Quay with a load of timber for J.D.Qualtrough, the local timber merchant. Most timber now is imported to the island by road transport from the UK using the Steam Packet Ro-Ro service.

This photograph of the **mt Helen** is another of my personal favourites. It was a regular visitor bringing fuel to Douglas during the 1960s. Although the pier was closed to the public during discharge, it was possible to use the walkway on the top of the pier to access the end of the pier and it was from this position that this photograph was taken.

There was a considerable export of livestock throughout the decade following the outbreak of foot and mouth in the UK in 1967. The island was, and still is, proud of its disease free livestock and was, at that time, in demand for store animals. Here the **mv Lincoln Express** is loading at the cattle steps on the Battery Pier in June 1976. It had been to the island in 1970 as the **mv Joanna Buitelaar**.

The Ramsey Steamship Co.'s *ss Ben Maye* was the last steam coaster purchased by the company. It was also the last operated by the company long after it had started the conversion to motor vessels. It is photographed in Castletown during October 1964, just two months before it was sold for scrap and broken up.

The *mv Lady McGowan* arriving at Ramsey to discharge explosives on one of the vessels regular calls.

There are several photographs of the Trans-Kosan liquefied gas carriers throughout these pages. They were very colourful and regular visitors to Douglas bringing lpg from the refinery at Milford Haven. Here is the *mt Helle Tholstrup* leaving Douglas on a typical winter departure.

The coasters bringing timber from the Baltic always added a splash of colour to the harbour scene as many had brightly coloured hulls. The *mv Peter Saxberg* is typical of many and was photographed in the late afternoon at Douglas.

Two for the price of one as the *mv Ben Vooar 3* leaves Douglas ahead of the inward bound *mv Ben Veg 2* photographed from the end of the Battery Pier.

Coasters belonging to F. T. Everard & Sons Ltd were regular visitors to the island for more than two decades carrying coal for the power station and later bringing bulk cement and the occasional load of fertilizer, *mv Centricity* was typical of those that came to the island during the 1960s.

As the Ramsey Steamship Co. vessels carried most of the domestic bulk cargoes to the island it is not surprising that they feature large in this collection. The crews were certainly good seamen and sailed in all weathers, as witnessed by this departure of the *mv Ben Varrey 3*.

The *mv Marianne C* arriving at Douglas in 1989 to discharge timber at the Victoria Pier. Coasters bringing timber from the Baltic were getting larger and were carrying part loads for discharge at several ports around the UK. They were no longer able to access the inner harbour and being larger were able to carry greater loads within their holds avoiding the hazards created by deck cargoes.

Here is an unusual photograph by any standards. The coaster *mv Claudia-W*, which was later to become the *mv Auldyn River*, for Mezeron shipping, is berthed alongside the promenade wall at Douglas unloading steel piling for the islands central sewage scheme, which involved constructing a large system of storage tanks under the promenade.

I have included a number of photographs showing some of the activity connected with the herring industry. This incident concerned one of the coasters, the Norweigan *mv Simla*, which was being used as a factory ship for processing the herring as the fishing fleet moved around the coast of Britain. It ran aground on the foreshore at Douglas at midnight on Saturday 12th November 1970. It was successfully towed off the following day.

The *mv Anne Ursula* was a German registered coaster with a load of timber for J.D.Qualtrough, timber merchants of Castletown. It is being discharged by one of the Harbour Board's mobile cranes at the Umber Quay.

The 300 ton Danish coaster *mv N.O.Petersen* registered in Marstal discharging timber at North Quay, Douglas.

The Dutch livestock carrier *mv Frisan Express* belonging to Rederij 'Frisan Express' is at the Battery Pier cattle steps in 1970 at the height of the herring fishery. Not only are cattle being loaded, there are full barrels of salted herring waiting collection but there are also bags of scallops on the quay. Astern of the coaster, there are two German trawlers engaged on the herring fishery.

Yet another lpg tanker vessels - the 300ton *mt Marina Tholstrup* arriving in April 1969 with liquefied gas for Douglas gas works to discharge at the Tongue in the inner harbour. The tanker was only three years old, typifying the infancy of this trade.

The importation of liquefied gas increased dramatically and by the early 1970s these tankers became the most frequent traffic in Douglas inner harbour. The largest of the Kosan vessels to use the inner harbour was the 390 ton *mt Signe Tholstrup* which was 60m long and could not turn at the Tongue and would be warped down the harbour and turned in the double corner or opposite Fort William.

Here the *mt Signe Tholstrup* is being turned opposite the Fort William berth which, by this time, was no longer used for the discharge of petroleum products.

The usual vessel on this run was the **mt Helle Tholstrup** and that is why it appears so frequently in this collection It ran in all weather as this photo shows.

Harbour maintenance was carried out by the IOM Harbour Board using their own personnel and the elderly steam grab dredger **sgd Mannin**. She is seen here placing anchors for the yacht mooring bouys in the Croak at Douglas. The diving boat **Perragh** is also in attendance and you can see the top of the diver's helmet just ahead of the tender.

The IOM Highway Board, who were responsible for the maintenance of the island's roads, also ran a quarry near Peel. When the local gas works stopped producing tar, the highway authority had to use bitumen which up to 1975 had to be brought in barrels from Stanlow. In this photograph the *mv Alfred Mason* is discharging barrels at the East Quay, Peel. This small coaster owned by John Tyrell of Arklow, had been built in 1919 and was reaching the end of its life.

Although I have already included a photograph of the *sgd Mannin*, I have included this phoptograph as it was almost at the end of its time with the IOM Harbour Board, who had already ordered a replacement to carry the same name, hence the suffix 2. It shows off the classic lines of the dredger as it leaves Peel in a northerly swell.

This photograph was taken in 1971 showing the *mv Ben Veg* turning within the confines of the inner harbour at Laxey having discharged grain for the flour mills. The harbour was closed to commercial traffic shortly after and all grain was discharged at Ramsey and taken by road to Laxey.

During the mid sixties and to the mid eighties the herring fishery was active in the Irish Sea after a gap of many years and already the activity at Douglas and Port St. Mary has been illustrated but activity was also present at Peel as this photo of Peel breakwater shows. Barrels are being unloaded and taken to the fish yards further up the harbour.

A regular complaint received by the island's coal merchants was that the coal that they were selling was full of slack. In fact my mother in law's coal merchant, when faced with such complaint, would reply "ay Elsie, its only fit for burning".

Like W.A.Mackie so many years earlier, I was fortunate enough to make a passage on one of the Ramsey Steamship Co.'s vessels. My trip was to Garston in July 1966 on the *mv Ben Veg* for coal and having witnessed first hand coal being loaded from railway wagons into the hold at the coal tips, it wasn't surprising that there was a lot of slack! The top photo shows the *mv Ben Veg* behind the *mv Saint Colman* waiting its turn on the tips.

The lower photograph was taken on passage approaching Ramsey with the AB Mike Spenser going forward to prepare the ropes for berthing at Ramsey.

The Dutch livestock carrier *mv Johanna Buitelar* loading cattle at the Battery Pier cattle steps in July 1972. The vessel was built in 1952 as the *mv Vechtstroom* and it had made a similar trip in November 1970. It also appears again in the colour plates as the *mv Lincoln Express*.

The Danish *mv Lindholm* entering Douglas inner harbour in the summer of 1972 with another load of timber. Even in the summer these small coasters could experience heavy weather and their deck cargo was always susceptible to shifting if not stowed correctly.

The German registered coaster *mv Birte O* discharging timber in the inner harbour at Douglas. The whole of the North Quay is now pedestrianised.

The new grab dredger *mgd Mannin* arrived in time to complete the work started by its predecessor at Peel. It is photographed dredging the breakwater berth which was regularly used by coastal tankers and importantly by passenger vessels of the IOM Steam Packet Co. when diverted from Douglas by easterly gales.

The Ramsey Steamship Co's *mv Ben Veen* leaving Douglas late in 1971 shortly after its acquisition from General Steam Navigation Co. Ltd. where it had operated from new as the *mv Plover*. At the time, it became the largest vessel to be operated by the local company.

The *mv Gerda Maria* was a frequent visitor during the herring season. On this occasion the coaster has had to anchor in the North Bay at Douglas to vacate the Battery Pier to allow a tanker to discharge. Of interest in the background is the White City amusement park still operating on Onchan Head with the roller coaster still in place.

The Norweigan tanker *mt Fostraum* of K/S A/S Straumtank was on charter to Shell during the early part of 1971 and was less than a year old at the time.

The coaster **mv Lune Fisher** owned by James Fisher, is typical of many similar charters brought on to handle the Isle of Man Steam Packet Co.'s freight traffic whilst their principal cargo vessel **mv Peveril** was on annual survey. On this occasion, in 1973, the company was well into its phase carrying containerised traffic and had erected a 28 ton Butters derrick crane on its cargo berth to handle it.

Not a coaster but I have included this photograph to show a typical winter scene off the mouth of Douglas harbour. Early in the year during winter gales, it was not unusual to find foreign trawlers legitimately fishing off the south east of the island, having to run for shelter at Douglas.

The Danish coaster *mv Salthammer* unloading timber at Ramsey East Quay for Corlett Sons & Cowley, a Ramsey timber merchant. The vessel's home port was Nekso on the island of Bornholm in the Baltic Sea.

The ice strengthened East German *mv Denebola* was photographed at Peel Breakwater on 14th January 1974.

Another coaster with timber at Douglas in October 1974. This time the three hatch Danish coaster *mv Fionia* from Odense on the island of Fyn. It is unloading on the north side of the King Edward Pier waiting for the tide before entering the inner harbour. It was indicative of the trend in the coasting trade towards bigger ships.

Late in the afternoon and the tide has risen sufficiently for the *Fionia* to make her way up to the inner harbour to complete the discharge of her cargo.

One of the regular exports in the 1970s from Castletown was scrap metal from a scrap metal merchant situated less than two miles from the port. Here the Cyprus registered *mv Chwinge* of the Ubique Shipping Co. is being loaded with scrap by an electromagnetic grab.

Still with timber imports and the Danish coaster *mv Greif*, one of the larger three hatch coasters employed on the trade by 1976, discharging in Douglas inner harbour. The fact that the vessel made two trips in 1976 also reflected an upturn in the building industry on the island.

The building industry is always a good barometer of the economy of a place and non more so than in an island situation. The matter was confirmed by the re-appearance of Everards larger modern coasters on the bagged cement trade from Gravesend. The 633 tons *mv Commodity* is photographed unloading at the Coffee Palace berth, Douglas in December 1977.

Not a coaster but I just couldn't resist including this photograph. The beautiful lines of the Northern Lighthouse Board's tender *mv Fingal* are seen to advantage as the vessel approaches the Victoria Pier, Douglas. If they were delivering s stores for the lighthouse they would usually be transferred by small boat from the tender standing off Douglas Head. A change of personnel, as witnessed by the furniture removal van on the pier on this occasion, would require berthing alongside one of the piers. The lights around the coast of the island are maintained by the Commissioners of Northern Lights not Trinity House.

In January 1976 the Ramsey Steamship Co. acquired more second hand tonnage and renamed the coaster *mv Ben Ain*. It had been the *mv Gretchen Weston* and it now became the company's largest vessel and served them well through a difficult period in the coasting trade. The coaster is entering Douglas harbour between the Edward Pier and the Fort Anne Jetty in April 1976.

Staying with the Ramsey Steamship Co., I have included another shot of the *mv Ben Veg* making a lively departure into a southerly swell. It is now almost impossible to photograph any ship leaving Douglas like this due, to the extension of the breakwater at Douglas.

Coastal tankers remain the regular coastal trade to Douglas and there are now an even greater variety of vessels bringing petroleum products to the island. One thing is certain, the tankers were getting bigger and we thought when the 982 ton *mt Partington* came on service that they were big!

This unusual vessel accompanied the Dutch fishing fleet on its journey around the British Isles. It was the Hospitaal - Kerkschip *mv De Hoop* photographed leaving Douglas. A number of local enthusists were able to inspect the facilities offered by this ship which included a fully equipped hospital, an equally impressive engineering workshop capable of carrying out major engine repairs and a recreation room which doubled as a chapel.

The *mv Mountcrest* was another coaster chartered by the IOM Steam Packet Co. to cover for the *Peveril* on annual survey during January 1977. It has turned around the head of the King Edward Pier and is being 'walked' back up the harbour to the Steam Packet cargo berth.

The 559 ton coaster *mv Candourity* of D.J.Goubert Shipping Ltd and managed by F.T.Everard on the cement contract, sailing through Douglas outer harbour after discharging another load of cement for local builders merchants.

The Shell tanker *mt Shell Engineer* arriving at Douglas in the tail end of a southerly gale in November 1979. She was new and representative of the larger tankers entering the coastal trade. The tanker was a regular visitor up to the mid 1980s - it was the era of the 1000 ton tankers.

J. & A. Gardner's vessels were no strangers to the island both for general cargo services and specialised heavy loads before the advent of Ro-Ro. The *mv Saint Kentigen* was photographed arriving at Douglas in April 1978 with the final pressure tank for the storage of liquefied gas to be located at the Battery Pier yard. The building of Ro-Ro facilities had commenced at Douglas and soon coasters with cargoes such as this would be a thing of the past.

Manx Line started a Ro-Ro service between Heysham and Douglas in July 1978, but by December had suffered catastrophic damage to their linkspan putting the service out of action for several months. Anxious not to loose recently hard won business a number of coasters were chartered to maintain the service with container traffic and *mv Pool Fisher* and *mv Eden Fisher* were two of them. Here is the latter entering Douglas.

The *mv Lady Mary* discharging timber at the Umber Quay, Castletown.

Early in 1981, IOM Shippers, a small shipping company operating between Peel and Northern Ireland, acquired the small 250 ton coaster *mv Thomas Grant* photographed unloading at West Quay, Peel. This vessel was built for the RMAS as a stores carrier but was later converted to a torpedo recovery vessel. In its guise as a coaster, it found a less arduous existence.

The French trawler *Le Croize* entering Douglas for shelter even though the harbour was closed due to easterly gales. Even the harbour master shouting 'Go to Peel' over the harbour tannoy did not deter them! It does clearly show the exposed nature of Douglas outer harbour to easterly gales before the new breakwater.

Now the next generation of 2000 ton tankers had arrived and one of the first was Everard's *mt Authenticity*, seen at the Battery Pier discharging fuel oil for the Pulrose power station.

The *mt Lotta Kosan* similarly represented the next generation of specialised liquefied petroleum gas tankers bringing butane to the island for Manx Gas. In their turn they too were to suffer from the pace of change when the island changed to piped natural gas.

Economies of scale forced the small coasters out of the Baltic timber trade by the 1980s and the vessels used were modern and generally far too big for the small ports of the island. Typical amongst these was the *mv Melton Challeger* seen discharging a part load of packaged timber at the King Edward Pier, Douglas in May 1981 for Qualtroughs of Castletown taking a part load of timber from the Finnish port of Valko The first port of discharge being Drogheda and the balance at Douglas.

Now Swedish timber is imported from the port of Kahja to Hull and then by road to Glasson Dock for shipment by Ro-Ro to the island with Mezzeron Ltd acting as agents.

The *mv Sea Thames* discharging coal at the Coffee Palace berth in Douglas inner harbour for National Fuel Distributers as the NCB depot had become known by this time.

From time to time scrap metal is exported from Ramsey. The local scrap metal merchants tend to store scrap until the price for scrap makes export viable. Here, in 1984, the *mv Skellig Rock* is loading at Ramsey.

The *mv Cecilia* turning at Ramsey in September 1984 prior to discharging explosives. The container on deck contains detonators.

To illustrate the capricious nature of the sea, the *mv Dego* was photographed arriving at Douglas in June 1983 when you would expect the weather to be calm. A southerly swell after gales from that quarter always subjected the approach to Douglas to a beam sea, although it was improved after the approach channel was dredged following the new breakwater construction.

Here is another of Gardners specialist coasters *mv Saint Brendan* discharging coal at the Office Berth, Douglas, illustrating the versatility of these coasters, designed as multi-purpose vessels which have been shown not only capable of handling general bulk cargo, but also heavy loads on their strengthened hatch covers.

On April 4th 1989, Merlin Manx Containers also started a rival freight service to the IOM Steam Packet Co. between Douglas and Belfast and the first signs that the new company meant business was when the *mv Fortuna Coast* arrived at the Victoria Pier, Douglas. The vessel arrived with a deck cargo of trailers with Lancashire flats and cargo in the hold, complete with its own cargo handling gear.

In November 1984 the *mv Ben Varrey 3* of the Ramsey Steamship Co. suffered a major engine failure on passage from Northern Ireland to Peel and was towed into Ramsey where it lay for sometime. Within a year it was decided that it would be scrapped. On the 15th September 1985, it was towed to Millom by the tug *Primrose* of the Laxey Towing Co.

Mezeron Shipping in Ramsey have owned and operated a surprising variety of coasters in their short existence.
The *mv Silver River* and *mv Subro Vixen*, which was to become Mezeron's *mv Colby River*, are berthed in Ramsey at Christmas 1986.

The *mv Saint Angus* arrived at the Victoria Pier, Douglas in August 1987 with a diesel generating set for Pulrose power station together with a heavy lift crane and this despite a fully fledged Ro-Ro service being in operation. The whole assembly was discharged at the Victoria Pier over the front ramp.

A National Union of Seamens strike which affected the IOM Steam Packet Co. saw a number of companies seize an opportunity to run rival freight services. One was Merlin Freight Services (later Merlin Manx Containers Ltd). This is the *mv Tara Ace* discharging containers and flats at the Coffee Palace Berth in the inner harbour at Douglas.

The German coaster *mv Gesche* is being assisted out of Douglas inner harbour by Laxey Towing Co.'s tug *Salisbury* as it was too long to turn within the harbour. The coaster, registered in the port of Rendsburg on the Keil Canal, had discharged a cargo of clay.

Another firm quick to seize an opportunity to find business on the island was Glenlight Shipping Ltd and they set up a local company Glenlight Manx Ltd and placed a number of vessels on the Manx shipping register. This is the *mv Glenfyne* of Glenlight Manx Ltd with a palletised cargo at Douglas.

More action in June 1995 at the King Edward Pier as the *mv Ala* discharges timber for the Douglas timber merchants. The following year timber was being off loaded at Hull and travelling by road and Ro-Ro to the island. It was almost the end of an era for coastal shipment of timber.

The coastal trade with petroleum product tankers on the other hand is as strong as ever. An occasional visitor during 1995 was Whitaker Tankers *mt Whitkirk* which was one of the smallest.

Mezeron Ltd went through a period of expansion during the mid nineties and acquired their largest coaster. Purchased as the *mv Tora* it was soon renamed in the corporate style of the company as *mv Greeba River*. It was photographed on 3rd June 1996 alongside the fitting out berth of the Ramsey Shipyard in its home port.

The *mt Fenja Kosan* makes her approach to the Battery Pier, Douglas to discharge another load of liquefied petroleum gas to the storage tank at the Battery Pier. Despite the island being connected to a natural gas supply for Douglas, the out towns still rely on butane air plants for their gas manufacture.

Ramsey Steamship's coaster *mv Ben Vane* discharging coal at Peel in March 1997.

In October 1999, the Ramsey Steamship Company acquired their largest coaster, the 997 ton Dutch vessel *mv Triumph* and on delivery renamed it the *mv Ben Varrey* becoming the fourth to carry the name in the company's eighty six year history. It is photographed leaving Ramsey shortly after delivery.

Another cargo of fuel oil for the newly established Total Oil depot being discharged by *mt Brentwood* at Peel Breakwater in April 2000.

Douglas inner harbour will never be the same as it appears in the photographs at the start of this collection. The reason being that it is now closed to commercial traffic and is a yacht marina. A water retention scheme completed in 1999 sealed its fate. The floating crane **Mersey Mammoth** is photographed on 30th March 1999 in position and

The Rostock registered *mv Lass Neptun* arriving at Douglas in December 2001 with general cargo to discharge at the Office Berth.

The large number of of capital projects in progress on the island over the last two decades saw a great variety of large coasters arriving with heavy items of plant and specialist equipment. The 3895 ton *mv BBC Mexico* was one of the largest and self discharged on the 21st August 2002 at the north side of the Victoria Pier. Each of its cranes were capable of lifting 80 tons or 160 tons in tandem. Managed by BBC Chartering and Logistic the vessel, which was built in 2001 was registered in Antigua & Barbuda.

The Dutch registered *mv Jaguar* discharging engineering equipment at the Victoria Pier, Douglas in May 2002

Among the vessels arriving with more specialised equipment was the low air draft *mv RMS Aramon* photographed in February 2003 approaching the Battery Pier, Douglas.

One of the next generation of Kosan tankers the **mt Lotta Kosan** at the Battery Pier on 9th March 2003 built in Germany and registered in the UK it is 73.6m long o/a and has a gross tonnage of 2213 – a far cry from the **mt Regitze Tholstrup** and the other 300 ton lpg tankers that first came to the island.

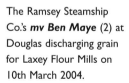

The Ramsey Steamship Co.'s **mv Ben Maye** (2) at Douglas discharging grain for Laxey Flour Mills on 10th March 2004.

The Isle of Man Steam Packet Co. needed to charter additional tonnage in June 2007. This was occasioned by the huge volume of vehicles and freight that came to the island for the celebrations of the centenary of the TT motorcycle races. Among the several vessels chartered during that time was the *mv Hoburgen* which was typical of those employed. It is seen turning in the outer harbour at Douglas preparing to drop onto one of the linkspans.

On the face of it just another Everard tanker but my how things have changed. In 2006 F.T.Everard was sold to James Fisher and the *mt Speciality* seen here at the Battery Pier operates under the James Fisher Everard banner. The tanker heralded an even newer class of tanker. It was less than a year old when photographed on the 18th March 2007 and was built at Wuhan in China its length o/a is 95m and it has a gross tonnage of 3859.

The *mv Ben Maye* and *mv Ben Ellan* of the Ramsey Steamship Co. in their home port of Ramsey over the Easter period 2008. I have included this photograph because it shows that the coasting company with which we started this collection is still going strong into the 21st century and still very much part of the island's coasting scene.

The introduction of Ro-Ro sevices to the Isle of Man has virtually killed off the coastal trade at Douglas. It still exists at Ramsey where Mezeron Ltd still carry break bulk cargo from the North of England and Northern Ireland, although they now have a number of 15m trailers and prime movers which use the Steam Packet Co. Ro-Ro sevice. The bulk cement contract currently with the Ramsey Steamship Co also guarantees trade. By way of contrast it seemed appropriate to end this collection of coastal shipping with this photo of the *mv Triumph* arriving at Douglas for berthing trials to cover for the *mv Ben My Chree* whilst it is on bi-annual survey.